Open Book
Open Soul

Gabrielle Hibbert

Poetry

First Printed in United Kingdom 2019

Published by Conscious Dreams Publishing
www.consciousdreamspublishing.com

ISBN: 978-1-912551-56-9

Dedication

Openbook, Opensoul is a window into my soul.
A delicate gift from me to you.
I dedicate this book to those on a journey of self-healing
and self-love.
To those who are afraid to confront the past and be open
with their pain.

May you be empowered!
Light & Love
x

Contents

To a soul who is seeking
I send out peace and light to you
May your spirit be blessed
As I express my test
A testimony of my journey...

I can't feel it!

At a glance, my beating heart was ripped from my chest
Disconnected without warning!

As I swallow back the dark truth, my heart beat accelerates...
Bleep
Bleep
Bleep
Bring my heart back!

As I shut myself off from the world and lie numb
Small rays of sunlight attempt to pierce through the
barricaded curtains
But I see no light, just darkness.

I feel no warmth
No heartbeat
Numb
Lifeless
Cold

Is it still there...MY HEART?

My eyes glaze over
Defeated
Drowning
Desolate
Absent in time and space.

As I gaze into his dark brown eyes for reassurance
I dive into an ocean of uncertainty & lies.

Hope fades away
Like a casualty and a victim entangled by fear
Helpless
Bring my heart back!

Tears fall to an unfortunate fate
Days fold over into years
All the memories dissipate into dust
Tears freeze over
And the harsh reality glares back at me.

BROKEN
&
BETRAYED BY LOVE!

As my body falls into a state of shock
I can't feel it beating...
MY HEART

Is it still there?
Knock, knock...No answer!

– Bring My Heart Back

Daily, my eyes weep, seeking a new home for the hurt...

I can't close my eyes at night when I lay to rest
Don't leave me alone
Betrayal
   Hurt
      Hate
Has consumed my spirit
Haunted by my past.

As I lay to rest, my soul shakes
Tears seep through my soft skin
My spirit is restless.

I fear to close my eyes and be alone with my dark deepest
thoughts
I am disturbed by the skeletons in my closet.

I bow my head down low
So no eye can connect with my spirit because it's shaking!

Don't look at me too long
You may meet my inner monster which I try so hard to keep
chained down
Don't look at me too long
You may meet my inner monster which I try so hard to keep
chained down!

Betrayal
    Hurt
        Hate
Has consumed my spirit

I can't close my eyes at night when I lay to rest
Disturbed by...

Betrayal
    Hurt
        Hate

– Haunted By My Past

I
can
see
beyond
your
mask.

A mask you wear to shield your heart
Your armour fit for a battle
A battle called love.

Why do you wear that hard cold glassed mask?
All I desire is everlasting dreams
Bodies entwining
Interlocking as one
That beyond the moon and back kind of love
Catching every star on the way!

But you repel my love
Retracting not attracting
Opposites attract they say...

– *Beyond Your Mask*

Fear
That capsulising emotion that takes over your soul
As the heavy raindrops beat down heavily on a dark night
My beat gets faster, faster, faster...I'm afraid
("Don't be")
Fast, ferocious, forsaking
Fear
Past, present, future
PAST
Undo!
Can't be (I'm afraid)

I am present but stuck in the past
My past has captured me
I'm held hostage by my fears
The fear of what is to come next
Will I ever be present in the present or be kept prisoner
to my past?
Will my body ever feel a warm touch again, will my heart
ever open up it's gates for love to flow through?
The future is unknown
I am afraid!

– *The Fear Of The Unknown*

I have no home
No place of contentment
No refuge

As a new day arises
I question...Who am I? Who was I?
Another day to face with an unfamiliar face
Unrecognisable

Who's that?
That's you
(Not me)
Lost!

Help me, call 999
I have an infection known as lost love
An infection which consumes my whole being
Seeping deep into the surface of my skin into the root of my soul

Who's that?
That's you
(Not me)
Lost

Like a spider
I crawl in and out of a web of confusion
Hanging onto a thread of hope
Unknown of which way to turn
Left, right
Right, left

Around and around I go
Left, right
Right, left
Around and around I go
Lost

How can I get off this ride they call life
I'm sick!
Like a rollercoaster, life brings more twist and turns;
So, I buckle myself up and brace myself for the next destination

Happiness, love, peace, death, disappointments, pain
Up
Down
Up
Down...
CRASH!

I witness an empty soul standing at a crossroad
Helpless
So I make it my mission to find my missing pieces
I begin to wonder amongst these tetris streets searching for
a new route
A new pathway that will lead me back to peace
Lead me back home

– L.O.S.T.

Protected
Preserved
Full Of Passion...
The strong yet cold iron bars shield her heart from the
arrows of sorrow
She patiently waits for the right key to unlock her precious
heart
She is locked in.

– *A Caged Heart*

Searching
Seeking closure
But how do you close the door on pain?
I seek clearance of these looming skeletons in my closet

Time has passed

But bittersweet memories have formed a web
in the corner of my mind
Pain hangs heavily on the door knob
Pain hangs heavily on the door knob
So close the door behind you
Close the door behind you
Don't leave your baggage here with me
I don't want it!
I don't need it!
I won't have it!
Close the door!

Open
Swaying
Back and forth

A gushing wind flies back to remind me of what could have been
My feet getting deeper and deeper like quick sand
Deeper and deeper
Deeper and deeper
I can't see myself no more
As pain hangs heavily on the door knob

So close the door behind you
I don't want it!
I don't need it!
I won't have it!
Close the door!

– *Close The Door*

My pen bleeds emotions
Searching for a blank page to fill with heavy words
From a heavy heart

My pen bleeds for a purpose
To create a special story...

– ***Bleeding Pen***

I swallow the pain I dare not endure!
As I lay to rest
Pain erupts and spills over into my dreams...
But
STILL
I Rise

I swallow the pain I dare not endure
I suppress the emotions which I can't express
But
Still
I RISE!

– *Resilience*

As I turn the page...
I say farewell to my friends
Goodbye to my comforts
Goodbye to the blanket that kept me warm
Goodbye to my refuge that kept me when the ground
beneath me was shaking.

Bags of tears fall
Bags of tears fall
Head up!
Deep breath!
Turn the page...

– Next Chapter

As the clock strikes 12
The past 365 days flash before my eyes
Like a flicker of light
It's gone!

I am enlightened
I am no longer the same
All that was written down in my book of life is now history
A distant memory to add to my archives of enriching
experiences
All that awaits now is a blank page
Blank page.

A new page
Fresh
Untouched
Awaiting to be filled with new adventures.

The last minute
Hour
Week
Shoots up into the black night sky to watch me from a
distance
Forming a rainbow of hope
Forming a new sparkling star in my colourful canvas of life
A blank page to start a new life
A blank page for me to write my story
My story I wish to tell....

– *New Year's Eve*

Cher Paris,
As I saunter freely through your beautiful streets
My spirit is enlightened
My soul is lifted by the love in the air
From the passionate lovers filling the evening nights.

City of Love, you present me with a gift so perfect and
intricate
Your magnificent tower radiates amongst the entire city
Overwhelmed
I stand in owe of you.

City of Love, thank you for opening my eyes and my heart
again
Now I am free to explore
Embrace all that comes my way.

City of Love, thank you for your elegant character and
demure nature
So, until the next time...
Au Revoir!

– Cher Paris

Above & Beyond
Fly high above the clouds
Find a new home
New Wings
New Life
Time to fly high now!

– Fly High

To forgive can be a hard pill to swallow
A pill of acceptance
A daily dose is recommended to bring me back to life
To ease the bitterness
To ease the burning sensation I feel when your name is
uttered.

Imperfection seals us together
Betrayal tore us apart
But forgiveness is the destination.

With no A to Z or alternative route
I clutch onto faith
The healing is in process and forgiveness...
En route.

– *Forgiveness En Route*

Fresh air
New life

As I look back, I see the old me in the distance
And just like that
My soul is consumed by a new sense of freedom
A heavy weight begins to rise off my compressed lungs...

Gradually
Slowly
I inhale small shallow breaths
New life
Fresh air

Finally, I can breathe again
Finally, I see a new life!

– *Breathe Again*

Turn around to something new
Fresh
Enlightened
BRAND NEW!

Turn around
(Who me?)
Yes you!

As you spin around your soul renews
No longer wounded
But healed

Life is a rollercoaster
Strap up
Hold on TIGHT
Seat belt on
And prepare for the ride of your life!

What goes up
Must come back down
If you're not prepared
You'll soon hit a round about
AROUND
AROUND
AROUND...
In circles you go!

Turn around to something new
Fresh
Enlightened
BRAND NEW!

Turn around
(Who me?)
Yes you!

– Life Is A Rollercoaster

The days of hide-and-seek are over!
No more confining your spirit in four walls
No more living in a prison of fear
You was born a fighter
Designed to fly high and not lie low

Be brave, be fearless, be fierce
Be brave, be fearless, be fierce
Be brave, be fearless, be fierce

You are in the ring with yourself so let the battle commence
You'll be head to head
Eye to eye with your enemy
You are your only competitor
Fear is your obstacle!

This is a battle you can't run from
But a battle you will defeat!
Be brave, be fearless, be fierce
Be your own BFF
Today!

– *Triple F*

Amongst the chaos, she clings onto the fragile strings of her heart
A peaceful melody plays in her mind.

As the voices grow stronger and louder
She watches the wall of communication fall
And the overgrown weeds continue to block out the light.

But STILL amongst the chaos
She can be still
She can be quiet
And inhale all that surrounds her
and...
EXHALE HOPE!

– Hope

Rest in peace
The old me is dead and gone
There is no going back now as all is buried six feet under
Homeless
No place
No space for the old me
R.I.P.

No regrets
No tears
No goodbyes
Just hello!

As I lay all that was not my best to rest
And protest what is meant to be
I whisper
Goodbye
Sweet dreams
A new star is born

– Old Me R.I.P.

White and black is only the start of her rainbow
Not just one colour but a palette of history and depth
Versatile
Unique
Talented

Wife, mother, daughter, sister
To raise
Empower
Educate
She wears all the hats
She plays all roles
A Queen of the stage!

Her fragile wings flutter freely
Back and forth
Elevating to higher spaces.

Like a chameleon in the vast open land of life
She evolves and transforms
Showering the world with her radiant rays
A versatile being
A master of her own masterpiece.

A
Woman
Of
Many
Colours.

— *Womanhood*

A war has started inside
A fire ignited by a restless spirit
A tug of war

Love vs pain
Weighing heavily on your heart
Sparking fear in your soul
It's time to let it go!

There will only be one end.
Instant casualties and deep fractures are inevitable
Only healed by the right dosage of time.

Deep under all those layers you wear for comfort is POWER
Be bold!
A part of you will die
But part of you will be born again!

– Time To Be Born Again

To love again means
Stripping everything back
Naked
Like a delicate new born
Exposed and bare
Vulnerable yet precious
Emotions rare and raw
Skin too sensitive too touch
Yet so beautiful

To love again means
Openness
Transparency
Fresh emotions

What a beautiful risk it is ...
To love again.

– Love Is A Risk

Never remain stagnated!

Dwelling in dark water will only drown your inner beauty
So float above
And blossom

– Lotus Flower

In this exact moment in time...
The way in which the words on this page leap out to touch
your heart
And connect with your mind
The sounds of life outside comfort you in your loneliest hour
A smile welcomes you
A conversation connects you with others
A warm hand touches your soul
All of these are entwined
Woven together.

The smallest things can carry hope
The smallest things can carry life
Cherish them!

– It's The Small Things In Life That Matter

Dear Mind,

At times...

Be Still

Be Quiet

Be Positive

Be Evolving.

– *Restlessness*

Laughter Lifts Life!

– Laugh

A Lioness
Her soul caged
Clawing through her barriers
Reigniting her fire
She Is Breaking Free!

– Caged Lioness

My eyes bleed fire & rage
Get me out of this prison!

A
prison
called
the
past.

– Captivity

Self-love is a life line
No full stop
Just a pause
To capture your breath
And love yourself
It's time now

Growth is essential
Progress is paramount
So EVOLVE
Be the best version of you
That's a real destination!

– *Self Love*

Peace & Love
I wear it daily!

– Fashion With A Voice

As the calm river glides along freely my soul is soothed
As I inhale the pure ocean aromas I can feel my spirit cleansing
My eyes capture the grand mountain view
The exotic flowers litter the narrow side-streets with their
rare radiance
The sublime evergreen nature captivates my heart!

I am elevated
I am free
D.O.M.I.N.I.C.A
I
Am
Home.

– Home Visit

My spirit no longer settles in dark dusty corners
But bathes in the rays of a new day
Joy blossoms in the morning
And my spirit flourishes once again

– *Morning Rays*

Yearning...
To find a piece of myself which is pure
Untouched
Untainted by the superficial hands of today

Seeking...
For a home which is filled with natural aromas
Natural light
Natural life
To rejuvenate my dead skin
My buried roots

Searching...
For a home where my ancestors mothers protect the land
The nature

Missing...
A land where a long-lost daughter is welcomed back with
a sun-kiss
Blessing her lonely soul

After God is the Earth
D.O.M.I.N.I.C.A
My Homeland
Awaits My Return

– Homeland

Freedom
Expression
Freedom
Expression

Express yourself because your voice matters!

– Freedom

A Rare
Red
Rose
Pressed
But
Not
Crushed

– Preserved For A Purpose

My soul screams freedom for all the innocent souls, children, mothers,
future presidents and doctors held captive by war.

My soul screams freedom for all the souls lost by violence
Now free to fly to a peaceful destination.

My soul screams freedom for the souls fighting to keep their head above water
Fighting to keep their hopes above clouds
Their dreams alive.

My soul SCREAMS for all the souls chained down by racism
All those souls violated by a nation which needs to open their eyes and minds,
and see we are all unique pieces of one big puzzle!
We are all in this together
We can grow higher in unity & love

MY SOUL
SCREAMS
FREEDOM
IS NOW!

– *Voice For The Voiceless*

Restore the broken bitter hearts consumed by the past
Restore the falling families buried beneath the rumble of
heavy disappointments
And piece the fractured hearts and fragmented memories
Back together

Design a new picture not so distorted but clear and beautiful
Fill the missing holes with unconditional love
Calling out...
Restore
Unify
Heal

Restore
Unify
Heal!

– It's Time For A Restoration!

Captivating all in her presence with her radiant smile
Her spirit brings a touch of warmth to a cold heart
Her spirit flows freely touching souls
With her endless love
Speaking life into broken spirits
Her spirit is so unique
So powerful
Reach out and touch her now!

– Her Spirit

The smile you paint on bares weight
But painting it on uplifts you
Heavy and sweet
A small dose you take daily

The smile you wear (a pretence maybe) a remedy (a cure I'm
not too sure)
To cover up the stains of life
But a smile has power to comfort your soul
Provide water to the weltered roots of your spirit

A smile can pull you out of the dark
Uplift your spirit
A smile
Wear it!

– A Smile, A Cure

Throw it down
Shout it out
Write it down
Throw it down
Share the load
Just don't carry it
Make it your mission to be better not bitter!

– ***Writing Therapy***

Above the clouds
Fly high above the clouds
Find a new home
New Wings
New Life
Fly High Now...

– Fly

Words Saves Lives
So Poetry Lives
Expression not Suppression

No more compromises
Time is of the essence
Live Life
Expression not Suppression

Words carry life
So speak words of positivity & power!
Expression not Suppression

– The Power Of The Tongue

Gabrielle Hibbert

Out of nowhere a dead flame reignites!
Shaking my wall of resilience
Burning my insides
Ashes still remain

– A Case Of The Ex

Far away my mind travels to a location where only birds can
reach
High above all dark clouds!
The carefree stars lay asleep peacefully in an ocean of
darkness

...

My
Mind
Travels
To
A
Place
Of
Elevation

– Elevate

I don't hate you
I don't blame you
I don't judge you
We all lose our way
We all fall down
We all bleed from old wounds
That is what makes us human

I just pray
One day when it's me in pain
You'll see it that way...

– Self-Expression Is Healing

Scared to leave
Scared to love

– Catch 22

Gabrielle Hibbert

My skin begins to melt under the intense pressure
Breathe life into my soul!

– Deflated but not Defeated

We all seek a connection in this long line of life
Where disconnection and discontent go hand in hand
Like long lost lovers separated by the vacant ocean

Comfort
Open
Natural
Necessary
Ego
Communication
Touch

Something untouchable
Something unbreakable

– ***Connection***

Emotions
They carry butterflies
Deep down into a pit
To that very place you gave up on!

Emotions can carry heavy tears from long lost words
Lost moments.

Emotions
Beautiful yet so fluid
Dangerous and unstable
A blessing and a curse
Bitter and Sweet
An overpowering PARADOX!

– Emotions

King of Kings
A Queen awaits you
Royal and righteous
Proud and powerful

A Lioness in full form
So caress her silky firm coat
Ease her mind with your gentle touch
Protect her bold heart

Inspire
Ignite
Admire her entirely

Security is what she desires a real soul
Where love is not just a word which rolls off the tongue
carelessly
But LOVE which is created
Nurtured
Fulfilled
That forever kind of love
A Queen awaits...

– Dear King

Gabrielle Hibbert

I reminisce back...

Back to the passion that kept my heart on fire with desire for love.

The fragmented memories keep me warm on lonely cold nights.

Reminiscing relieves the pain
It's like you never left
It's like your still here
The pleasure & pain.

Seeing your face again brings comfort just for a spilt second
Until hate sparks up and drains out all the love
Leaving an empty shell.

The reality is...
You're gone
The love has gone
You hurt me
No more reminiscing
No more reminiscing

The past has already passed away
No more reminiscing
No more reminiscing
The past has already passed away

Time to let go of you now!

– Reminiscing

I have loved
Broken hearted
I was lost
But was rescued.

Transforming
I lost peace of mind
Weeds began to grow and choke me
I was greeted by my inner monster
What an ugly picture it was to see
Growing.

Dreaming
Aspire to be?
I was dedicated
Heart and soul
But was left disappointed
Learning.

Stagnant
Darkness was all I could see
Every second, minute, hour, day, week...
Another year
No change!

Light and dark
A ray broke through one January
But had no time to console me
Darkness captured every part of my being
Holding me hostage.

Confronting
My enemy
To torment
Tarnish
Destroy
Was their plan
A plan they failed to achieve.

Excelling
Lioness
Fighter
I choose to be!
Losing
Quitting
Not an option.

So to the woman I am destined to be...
I have
Loved
Lost
Died
Confronted
Excelled
Transformed
And
Now
READY TO CONQUER!

– To The Woman I Am Destined To Be...

Humanity In Harmony
Humanity Humanised
Holding Hands
I have a dream
A dream of peace & love.

– Peace & Love

Vibrate Higher
Feed your soul positivity
Self-care on a daily
You deserve to rise high!

– *Self-Preservation*

One love

In harmony
As one
UK
UNITED
In one
KINGDOM
In one
LOVE

– One Love

Dedicated to all the lost souls in the Grenfell fire
And the Manchester Arena bombing
Year 2017
RIP

P. ower
E. mpathy
A. ction
C. onnected
E. volve

– P.E.A.C.E.

Life
In full
In love
In abundance
A promise!

– Life Is Full Of Greatness

Dark, deep and heavy!
I can feel it suffocating me
Leaving me breathless at night...
BUT
Although my position seems restrained by unknown forces
My perspective is MIND over MATTER
You got this
YOU GOT THIS!

– *Anxiety*

It takes great strength to smile whilst your crying on the inside
A smile
A transparent plaster you put on daily to stop the pain from bursting out uncontrollably!
I know it hurts but your struggles today will be your strength tomorrow
Peace is waiting for you
Peace is waiting for you
Peace is waiting for you
Hold on!

– **Growing pains**

Soften your hearts and mouths today
Speak a word of love
We are all fighting our own wars
We all need a little tenderness

– *Compassion*

It's never too late to place a full stop in your line of pain
The writer of your destiny so hold firm onto your pen
Create a new pathway
To a day you dream to see

It's never too late to make that choice to change your direction
To set your mode to forward and not back
Up and not down!
No more around and around
But reset on your mask get set go!
It's never too late to rewrite your history
And retell a story you desire to read

It can never be too late to be born again
A fresh
A new thing
And fly to higher heights
Start something brand new
To live a life which you were designed to live

It's never too late!
Late is a concept of time
And time is in your hands
So make time to make a change now!

Remember it's never too late to create a new pathway
It's never too late to rewrite your destiny
To write a new story
A story which is brighter!

– *It's Never Too Late*

Dear Peace,
Where are you?
As I wonder aimlessly, I wreck my mind to find you
Can't breathe, can't see, can't move
All peace has left me
A prisoner to my own thoughts now
At war with my own flesh
Not a battle of man vs man
But body vs spirit.

Peace, Peace, Peace
Please where are you?
Where are you?
Not rhetorical but remains unanswered
I wait for a moment to just smile again.

Knock, knock, knock
I keep knocking!
Knock, knock, knock
I keep knocking!

Peace, Peace, Peace
Please where are you?
Peace, Peace, Peace
Please where are you?

I am here
I am God
Come find me...

– *Dear Peace*

Overwhelmed.
As I walk through the valley
Barley walking
Heavy-hearted
Mind crippled
I am overwhelmed with emotions
Brittle
Bruised
Branded
Exhausted.

Until now, the way has been dark & grey
I was lost in the valley
But the old me is fading away now.

– Silver Lining

Hurdle, run, hurdle
A race we begin with no head start
Just on your mark get set go!

Run before you walk
Walk before you crawl
Baby steps they say

As babies we race towards crawling
Race towards adulthood
But how do you survive in the hood as an adult?

Chase Peace, not P's
Chasing
Chase peace

The more we have
The more we want
The more we want
The more we chase...
Towards a finish line that has no ending

We come across hurdles in this race of life
But these are broken down by our maker
Because pain is temporary
And contentment is like a feather in the wind
Flying aimlessly

So what are you chasing?
Chase peace, not P's
Chase peace, not P's
Chasing...

Slow down
Take a breath
Lay back and comeback to yourself
Not chasing P's but finding peace within yourself
That's what's priceless

Stop chasing just for a minute
Stand still and flourish in the present
A master of your masterpiece

Strive for peace
To piece back together the broken parts
Evolve, exchange, elevate to a better place!
Chase peace.

Seek peace over material gain because money can't buy peace
Seek to keep your passion alive
Continue to chase your dream
Chasing peace not P's
Chasing
Chase peace.

– *Money Can't Buy Peace*

Behind my smile lies words I bury deep...
Deep in my soul to keep the rage from pouring out
Behind my smile lies a spirit unreleased

I paint on a smile to convince my soul I am not aching
Aching from the lies, betrayal, negativity

My smile carries heavyweight
Behind my smile lies a woman who has many layers
Many stories
Behind my smile lies history

My smile carries the burdens of the past
I paint on a smile to fight away the tears
But my heart is burning from the rage
Behind my smile lies a heavy weight.

– *Heavyweight*

I
Need
You

I need you to show me how to be strong
To teach me the lessons you learnt the hard way
To show me how to be strong
To teach me the lessons you learnt the hard way

I need you to touch the soft petals of my soul that need
tenderness
So I don't go hard
I need you
If only you could see that

I need you to teach me how to guard myself from the
disappointments of life
I need you to embrace me with love, so I know what love
feels like
I need you if only you could see that!

I need you to show me how to love myself
To love my scars
To love my insecurities
A mother-daughter kind of love

I need you if only you could see that!

– A Mother-Daughter Kind Of Love

Gabrielle Hibbert

Stop
Pause
Rewind
And freeze this very moment ...so I can breathe again
So I can process all these emotions which run through my
mind
Not leaving an archive in my memory but rather more
unanswered questions
More open wounds
I am imperfect
Perfection is unknown to me

I reflect on the last day, hour, minute
All the fragmented memories gather to the front of my mind
It's time to...
Re-evaluate
Redirect
Reshape
Perfect imperfections.

Rage may take over
Pain may take over
Past may take over
Life may take over
YES!
As I re-evaluate
I discover...

– Perfect Imperfections

Your life is a living letter so make every word count!

– *Live*

Like wine she matures with time
So, pour yourself a tall glass
Her succulent berries burst amongst confusion and confliction
Creating a deep rich flavour
Her tantalizing aromas will tease your taste buds
Her riches are worth more than gold
One taste and you will never be the same again
Transformed in body, mind & spirit
It will be worth the wait!

– The Wait

I have a bullet proof heart.
I have so many holes
That I have lost count on counting on absent lovers, mothers,
fathers...
Absent-minded

I have a bullet-proof heart.
False promises and unfilled expectations
All leave unforgiving holes which I crave to fill
Like a blank page awaiting the touch of a retired writer
I crave

My heart is not whole but contains holes
Resilient & beating hard
Now open again
By faith
Resilient & beating hard
Open again
By faith
I have a bullet proof heart!

– **Bullet Proof Heart**

Your body is a gift
Your body is art
A valuable
No label can define your worth
No fabric and no bond can contain your unique beauty
Your body is a temple for a King
A bridge of connection
A foundation in which greatness lies
Where the richest knowledge is buried

Your body can carry you to high places
But it needs love from you
No one else can fill that need but you

Your body is a gift to this world
Your body is art
Love your body
LOVE YOU!

– *Your Body*

As I swim through toxic waters
Waiting for sun-light to pierce through and comfort me...
I take a deep breath & pause.

New light
New day
New light
New day

I close my eyes and dream of the day when the water will be clear
Clear enough to see through and cleanse all
Cleanse the toxic pains and memories

So I wait.
Wait to bathe in a new day
A new light
A new day
A new light.

– Horizon

Amongst the wilderness
I grow new roots
Absorbing the strength from the land
Wild and free
I write
My voice shall not be buried but born again

Amongst the wilderness
I lay still and wait
Peace is due now

As I look back, dead memories stare at me
I confront the enemy breaking inside of me
And hold the pieces I dare not shed

Amongst the wilderness
I was lost and found
Amongst the wilderness
I found freedom.

– *Amongst Wilderness*

Dear Pain,

Why have you become so familiar?
Like an old school friend
You never seem to leave my memory
Lingering moments flash back
I overdose on positivity to try to drown you out, but your
power is just so intense.

I know you carry lessons with your weight, but at times you
perplex me with your spontaneous arrivals
You leave a bittersweet taste behind.

Pain...why do you choose to linger unnecessarily?
I guess joy is your rival
Pain without joy
Joy without pain
Causes one to lose power.

Dear Pain,
I am not your best friend, but I understand your role
Thank you for craving resilience into my bones
Thank you for teaching me how to appreciate joy and peace
I just ask one thing...
Please keep your power of de-sensitivity
Because although you hurt
I still need to feel.

Love From,
A Loving Heart
X

– *Dear Pain*

We need a revolution
Hate is the crime
And love is at stake

Let us revolt from the poisonous ways of society
Let us love with actions
As words are fickle and easily lost in the fabrics of life
Let us revolt from anger
Let us love with actions

We need a revolution
Hate is the crime
And love is at stake

We need a revival to revive our dead spirits and let a new
light reign
We need a revolutionary change
Because hate is the crime and love is at stake!

– Revolution

Gabrielle Hibbert

Imagine better days
They are coming hold on
Clouded by the darkness that is chasing them

Imagine better days
When home is not pain
But home is peace
Things are going to get better
Things are going to get better
Things are going to get better
Better days are due

You're trying to keep them hostage to a scene overplayed
Unhook the chains of the past
You're trying to keep them hostage to a scene overplayed
Unhook the chains of the past
Better days!

They are up for the test
Because every day they are blessed
So they put up a fight to live right
To fly to higher heights because their brothers missed the flight
But they will still rise with them
But they will still rise with them
Things are going to get better
Better days are due

As time goes by, they cry
As they lay down another soul
Another brother

Another mother says goodbye
BUT
It's too early to say goodnight to their dreams
So they are going to aim high
And tell a story together
Make this dream together
Tell a story together
Make this dream together!

To voice
To express
To speak into the lives who are dying
Not just for them but for their future brothers
Fallen kings

To speak life to death
Not just for them but for their future brothers
Fallen kings
How?
When tomorrow looms with today's sorrows...

But they trust in FAITH
They trust in FAITH
It's going to get better
Things are going to get better
Things are going to get better
Better days are due!

– Better Days Are Coming

I try so hard to fight the wrenching sensation that lays in my
stomach
Screaming for an escape
But I can't let it out
A wound
An open flesh exposed to all surroundings
To heal means to close
To repair
But how do you close something which is not linear but deep
Not simple but complex
Healing hurts

Who knew healing hurts
If only I could let emotions in
Long enough to fill the empty spaces and leave
But I am scared!

Scared to let the pain in
Scared that it may not leave
Scared that it may consume me like before!

– Healing Hurts

Who knew that you could re-live your darkest memories
Who knew that time could flash back?
Freeze and recreate this very moment
Déjà vu

The memories send shivers up to your fingertips
The thoughts pound at the side of your temple
Your mouth cannot comprehend this moment...this feeling
Déjà vu

Your heartbeat beats to a rhythm of uncertainty
Who knew déjà vu would reveal the answers to the questions
which lay ahead
A reoccurrence
A retelling
A coincidence
All draw to a singular moment in the past
Already lived, touched, experienced
Déjà vu

But God knows the past is a story already written
And the future is a story yet to live out
So let go of the past
And live in the now!

Fear creates barriers
A negative emotion creating negativity
You're an overcomer
So have faith
You were not born to remain in toxic waters
So live in the now

– Déjà vu

No false pretence
No bravado or false promises
Just sincerity

Tomorrow is not guaranteed
So let's take the now
And make it ours
Soul to Soul
We are One!

– Soul To Soul

S.T.R.E.N.G.T.H.
C.O.U.R.A.G.E.
W.I.S.D.O.M.

– A Daily Prayer

So many things on my mind...
But one day all things will be
beautiful again

– Occupied

Gabrielle Hibbert

Don't rush the process
Let Nature Run It's Course

– *Dating Game*

I am leaking
My eyes no longer pour but my heart still aches
Fill me up
Because something is missing
Bridge the gap between my heart and my spirit
Fill me up!

– Emptiness

Be my friend in time of need
Reliable
Right by my side
Be my anchor when I am sinking
My peace in time of chaos
My joy in times of pain
A rock of trust in doubt
My fighter in times of battle
A lover unconditionally
Be A Lover & Friend

– Lover & Friend

If it makes you smile
Make room for it!

– *New Space*

Be
My
Peace
I've
Had
Enough
Of
Pain
Face to face
Eye to eye
I
See
You
But
I
Am
Unbreakable!

– The Weakness In Me

I am trying to catch my breath
And process all these emotions that are running through my
mind...
Not leaving a picture in my memory
But rather a stream of unanswered questions
Fresh wounds
.O.P.E.N.

– Open Wounds

When we meet, I feel like we never drifted apart
In your vast absence
I am not alone but entwined
My mind is silenced
My spirit is settled
Connected to the one thing that has no end...no voice
A soul of it's own
I am one in your oar
My endless love.

– *The Sea*

Absence seeks presence
Presence seeks a connection
Connection requires openness
Openness is beautiful
And beautiful is you!

– Inner Beauty

He brought me this far
He pieced me back together when my heart shattered
Yes, I may fall
But not too far for he is ready to catch me
His heavenly wings comfort my restless spirit
His words speak life into my heart and all noise fades
He is my keeper!

– *The Most High*

Calling it quits is not in my calling.
But quitting calls me
As I approach the finish line
I hear a voice calling me back...
Back to back track me, to a script overwritten, overplayed, over!
Back to back track me, to a script overwritten, overplayed, over!
Quitting is not in my calling.

As I press towards the mark, pressure presses me, crushes me, pushes me
But I am pressing towards the mark
I am pressing towards the mark!

As I pursue towards my purpose, pressure calls me
Not to be overwhelmed by what's before my time
But to override what's not for me
And let be now
I am pressing towards the mark.

Calling quits is not in my calling.
But quitting calls me
As I approach the finish line
Pressing on persevering
A visionary on a mission
Ready for battle
Pressing on persevering
A visionary on a mission
Ready for battle!

I can see it now
No longer a dream but reality
A reality where peace & love is welcomed like a long-lost child
As I press towards the mark
Quitting is not in my calling
My life lessons of rising came wrapped in my falling
No time to for stalling,
Stepping up is the calling that winners never quit

My life lessons of rising came wrapped in my falling
No time to for stalling
Stepping up is the calling that winners never quit!

So...
I am pressing towards the mark now
I am pressing towards the mark now

I
AM
PRESSING
ON
NOW!

– Quitting Is Not In My Calling

Mind over matter not matter over mind
Seek what's in front and not what's behind
Look to your Maker because He is your Creator
Who keeps you from falling and hears your calling
Who keeps you from falling and hears your calling

Mind over matter not matter over mind
Because Mind
Matters
MIND
MATTERS!

Because he gave you a mind which is soundproof
So look to your future and strive high
As the lie of the enemy fails to provide what your life purpose
has to offer
The lie of the enemy fails to provide what your life purpose
has to offer
SO STRIVE HIGH!

Mind over matter not matter over mind
Mind
Matters
MIND
MATTERS!

Create a vision
Look to the Creator
And await a new pathway

Because it's all in His hands now
It won't be long now

Because it's all in His hands now
It won't be long now
So take a leap of FAITH
Because YOU CAN!

HE is in control
So, step into the role that awaits you
Because YOU matter
And your MIND matters
And YOU are FREE
And your MIND is FREE!

Mind over matter not matter over mind
Mind over matter not matter over mind

MIND
Matters
MIND
MATTERS!

– *Mind Over Matter*

('For God hath not given us the spirit of fear;
but of power and love,
and of a sound mind'
– 2 Timothy 1:7)

Talk positive to yourself
Encourage yourself
Believe in yourself
Be your own cheerleader!

– Talking Therapy

Remember to water your own flowers daily
So you can blossom
And your roots can grow deeper
Light & Love
Are the key ingredients

Empty your cup daily
Cleanse your mind
Refresh your soul
Be free in spirit
And wait
New buds are blooming

– *Mind Garden*

Petals
Fall
Fallen
Petals

Fall

Fall

Fall

Fall

Fall

Fall

As
The
Sun
Falls

Your authentic beauty still radiates
Don't grow weary now your seeds will blossom again

– Autumn

Be who you were created to be and nothing less!

– Purpose Driven Life

I am motivated by His Perfect Love
From Above
He puts to rest all!

– *Perfect Love*

Your rich in more ways than one
If only you knew your worth!

– Self-Worth

That sense of accomplishment
No words can describe it
That feeling keeps you driving
Keeps you ploughing through the darkest storms
With no sense of direction
Sometimes no sight
That feeling
That dream
Holds you
Keeps you
That day will come!

– Daydreaming

It's time!
Time to launch out now my beautiful butterfly
The world is waiting to be touched by your beauty
So, break out of your hard shell
And spread those colourful wings

It's time to fly!
Time to launch out now, my beautiful butterfly
Set your spirit free
You deserve it now!

– Metamorphosis

Like an onion,

I peel away the dead skin of my soul

Awaiting a new fresh layer of life

A new sense of freedom

– Shedding Season

YES, YOU CAN!
Because you are filled with a rare power
And your inner rainbow is rich
Powerful
Limitless
A conqueror

YES, YOU CAN!

– Fighting Talk

Enlightened...
As I delve deeper into my soul
I learn to embrace my beauty & my beast
My dark spots & bright highlights

– Self-discovery

Silence the negativity
And magnify the joyful moments
Life is what you make it!

– Perspective

Living water flow through our lives
Nourish the weltered roots of our spirits
Cleanse the dark water
And bring a new light
Living water flow...

– A New Flow

You are blessed to be a blessing
Someone is waiting on your story
Open your book and let your life be a blessing

– Life Story, A Life Support

Uncomfortability uncovers the undercover vulnerabilities of your soul.
To enter your vulnerable space is to touch an unsafe zone
Roam an unfamiliar home that you dare not loan your spirit too
Because your vulnerabilities hold power.

You wrap them away like a golden pearl maintaining it's worth.
But life can force you to touch those soft spots
And enter a zone of uncertainty
Life can force you to discover that power that lies within you
Your vulnerabilities hold power.

Fight fear with faith!
Find comfort in your uncomfortable parts, as pleasure derives from pain
And light flows through the dark holes
May your uncomfortability birth greatness and shine clarity on your vision
Embrace your soft parts
Because your vulnerabilities hold power!

– *Vulnerability = Power*

Dear Future,

I write into you, filling you with life and no blank spaces
May each day be filled with beautiful and enriching lessons
Filled with moments that speak volume in a silent room.

Dear Future,
I wish I could touch you.
But I dare not spoil your pure frame
You are filled with beautiful and ambiguous layers
So rich with history
I could never afford you
But your worth it!

Love From,
The Present
X

– Dear Future

May we teach our future generation that a star is NEVER too
high to reach
But a star lies WITHIN them
They are the PRIZE!

May we teach them VALUES
Show them LOVE
PRAISE them!

May we teach discipline
And spread
TRUTH & GRACE

May we teach them to be IN-DEPENDANT
And dependant on NONE

Instil humbleness in them
So they can reach a hand out to their fallen brothers and sisters

May we help them create a VISION!
A vision which will leave a trail in history
A vision which encompasses their uniqueness

May we teach them to wear PEACE & LOVE daily!
And show them how to bottle it up
So they have a cure at hand, in case they become sick from
the worries of life

May we TEACH them that they are UNBREAKABLE...
Because they are a RARE DIAMOND!

– Teach, Life Lessons

Dear Joy,

I adore thee
Want you open up like flowers
And birth a new life in me.
Cure my heart & soul with your pure light.

Joy,
You are a gift I wish to unwrap daily
Feeling your presence is a present I desire
May my soul dwell in you.

Love From,
A Lonely Heart
X

– *Dear Joy*

I was lost
I was found
I was lost
I was found

As I begin shredding the dead layers
I am neither lost nor found
But building new wings
New skin

As my soul dwells in peace
I wait patiently to fly to my dreams
Gaining balance & strength to pursue a testing way

Like a bird walking a tight rope, my wings grow mighty strong
And a divine power holds me
Gently pushing me ahead

I was lost
And
Found

– Finding My Way Out

Y
O
U

Y.O.U.
Are beautiful right where you are!

Acceptance
Approval
Accept you as you are right now

Because you are beautiful!

Embrace you
Wrap your arms around your soul
Give yourself some unconditional love
Celebrate the beautiful lessons as pruning season begins
Reside in a new space and reflect on your journey.

It's time to discover yourself again.
You are beautiful right where you are

Your shape is undefinable not linear
Unique & Original!
At the core of you is power that spirals out light
The destination is not the goal but to embrace the journey

At the core of you is power that spirals out light!
You have come so far
You have come so far

YOU HAVE COME SO FAR

You are beautiful right where you are!

– *Y.O.U.*

Build your wings to fly high
To reach your destination
To not miss any stars on the way
To not miss any stars on the way
Build your wings to fly high

Build your wings to rest in serenity
To find a home where love & peace paints the sky
You may be falling but your building your wings
You may be falling but your building your wings
You may be falling...
But you must grow to sustain the ride
Because you were designed to fly to your destination
To spread light to dark places
To spread light to dark places
To fly to a destination of elevation
To elevate high
To fly
Build your wings to fly
H.I.G.H!

– *Elevation*

Pursue
Your
Purpose
With
Passion

– Passion Is Your Driving Force

My cards have been dealt.
But I have the upper hand because He is in my corner
Making the next move
Making a new plan

I have the upper hand
Because the controller has a map which maps out a winning hand
The harder the game the sweeter the victory!

As I write my story back to glory,
I discover a new path...
...a pathway that even winners couldn't foresee
Something so sublime
Something so unreal

I have the upper hand
So, the next move is on me
To foresee what is not for my destiny
To be a winner not a victim
To take back what's mine
And define what winning is to me!

Attitude is the main ingredient in the recipe of success
So...
I am going to play the upper hand
And make the right moves towards the finish line!

I have the upper hand with God by my side.

– *The Upper Hand*

The hardest decision is the decision to make a change!
To become something unfamiliar
To become something brand new
To step out of the queue
Out of a line not set up for you
To make your mind up
To leave behind what you have out grown
Overthrown
Overstayed
As it no longer fits you
It no longer serves you

Change is a choice you can only choose in your time frame
But change creates growth
Is it time for a change?

– Made Up Mind

You are swimming in murky water
Not so clear
Not so clean

But clarity lies ahead in the distance
Can you see it?

Your pushing against the tide and your head is above the water...

Waiting

                                       Waiting

Riding through the waves

                        Wrestling with yourself

Wrestling with life Waiting

        But your vision will become clear!

Keep swimming

Keep pushing

Keep swimming

Keep pushing

Keep swimming

Keep pushing

Amongst the floating weeds, lies all the answers you seek...
So
Keep swimming
Clarity lies ahead!

– Just Keep Swimming

Joy
Comes in the morning
To eradicate fear
To eradicate the darkness of last night
Because fear distorts your view
Creates blind spots
Clouds your perspective
Be patient and persevere through
And learn to trust your season
Because love is always above us shining down

– Joy Comes In The Morning

Life is a cycle of change
Continuously moving
Continuously shifting
Transporting us through different cycles

So, as you enter a new season
May your seeds absorb new light
And may you continue to grow upwards

– Flourishing

As I take another step, guard my way
May each move be aligned with your plan
I am not the controller but the passenger on this ride,
awaiting instructions.

I know the road ahead will not be straight or smooth
But I am no longer blinded by fear but blinded by your light
I can now see clear.

I am excited about the next turn
The next discovery...

– Stepping Stones

Life is a blank page
Ready for you to fill up
In between the fine lines of life there is beauty to be
discovered
Knowledge to learn.

Wisdom withheld is worthless
So seek deeper in between the cracks
In between the chaos.

Red, brown, white, black, green
Are just some of the colours that may catch your eyes
But look closer!
There is always something happening
There is always something waiting to catch your heart
To take you to a higher level

So, believe there is someone out there waiting on your
breakthrough
And your perspective holds the key to a new life.

How we see life
Allow it to affect us
Even control us at times
Can determine whether we rise up or stay down
So, may your perspective be positive!

– Perspective

I commit my way onto Him each day
Learning to trust & lean on him more
I am humbled by His grace

– *God's Grace*

You are freedom
You are all & nothing at the same time
Simple Beautiful

Every time we reconnect, I feel alive again
Your motion moves my spirit to a place untouched
To a place my spirit can reside

You are freedom
You are all & nothing at the same time
You are simple beautiful

– *The Sea*

You are STRONG
You are ABLE
You are a FIGHTER
No longer I can't
But I AM
Speak words of power into your life!

– Self-Affirmations

Every time, at the same time
I cry
Help
Less, lesson, learning.

I cry
But my voice is drowned out by the white noise
The white noise of capitalism, corruption, consumerism
A green system which recycles the lives of the oppressed
screaming freedom
Every time, at the same time I cry for help.

As my last tear falls
I am no longer a victim but victorious
No longer helpless but powerful
No longer suppressed but expressed
Liberated!

The days of suppression are buried down under
A voice for the voiceless
I scream Freedom
I scatter seeds of victory amongst the land
And wait for greatness to rise!

– *Expression Not Suppression*

Falling
Seeking
Praying
For a safe landing, from a fall
Unexpected
Uncalled
I call out
Home, where are you?

To land
To be secure
To be still
Damage
Control
Alert

To land safely is a prayer I pray
To land safely is a prayer I pray
Because my fall is from a place of heights
Not mountain views but dark nights
Seeking
Praying
For a safe landing

Falling
Seeking
Praying
Falling
Seeking
Praying
Because I am sick & tired of being sick & tired
Of cycling in circles with no change!

Pain
Circle
Anger
Circle
Life
Full circle

But I don't know how to stop cycling & start walking
Or even stand still
Long enough to allow myself to feel
To accept where I am right now
To Land...
A place I desire yet fear
Because to land from my fall means acceptance
I will have to face the beast that I fight to conceal
And face the pain because I am hurting
To face the pain I conceal but I need to heal
Because I am hurting
To face the pain

Because I am hurting...
That's a real landing

As I fall
I pray
To find my home
To feel secure
To be at peace

Falling
Seeking
Praying

Falling
Seeking
Praying
For a safe landing!

– Landing

Arise my Kings & Queens
Fallen season is over
Rising is now

Fear has been your home for far too long
So perfect peace you deserve!

Arise my Kings & Queens
Do not be afraid no weapon shall prosper against you
Born a warrior
Fit to fight all battles

It's time to rise up
Fight back
Lift up

It's time to rise up
Fight back
Lift up

Celebrate & Believe
Because all the power is in the palm of your hands
What you touch shall bare roots if you trust it to grow

Falling season is over
Rising is now
Falling season is over
Rising is now
So RISE UP!

The way is already paved so take that step out NOW!
Your crown awaits
Time to radiate in your skin
Blossom in your gifts
Birth a new life

Arise
Arise
Arise
KINGS & QUEENS

Falling season is over
Rising is Now
Falling season is over
Rising is Now

So Rise Up!

– *Arise*

Saving Grace where are you?
Saving Grace where are you?
Saving Grace where are you?

I was saved from a destructive storm.

Deadly winds blew my mind
Tore all my inside, my thoughts had no place to reside
Alone
Isolated

I was saved for better days
To share with my brothers & sisters
To save them for better days
To live in peace and love
Saving grace

I was saved!

Death, absence, a numbness, a nothingness
A daily state I could relate
So I tried to medicate with toxic remedies
Not realising that I AM the cure to my disease
And my FATHER above prescribed a natural high
No recharge just a heavenly POWER

Saving grace, I was saved
Saving grace, I was saved
Saving grace, I was saved
Saved for better days!

Gabrielle Hibbert

I was saved at a time when no man's land was my home
Which I chose to roam
Signal failure
No light
Lost
No home
Empty

Until, I plugged into the live wire and reconnected to a higher source
High
Power
Saved
High
Power
Saved!

His grace begun to fill the broken holes with unconditional love
From above
A dove gracefully landed on death
And put to rest all!

I was saved for better days!
To share with my brothers & sisters
To save them for better days

To spread peace and love
To spread peace and love
To spread peace and love

I WAS SAVED FOR BETTER DAYS!

– *Saving Grace*

Art is...
Expression
Liberation
Love
Peace
Anger
Joy
Pain
Me
You
Us
Just one stroke and we are united!

As a combination of colours spread across a blank canvas
A new thing is created
Something diverse
Something unique
Just like me
Just like you
Just like us!

Art is...
Life
Alive
Culture
Identity
Freedom!

– Art Is

A.
Singular
Just like you
Enough
On your own

L.
Longing to be loved by someone
But love starts with you
Alone
In love
With you

O.
On your own
Ownership of your emotions
Of your body
Of your mind
Of your past
Of your weaknesses
O!

N.
Night time can seem darker alone
But teaches you to hold on tighter to those moments of light
The moments wrapped in love
The moments that catch your breath

E.
Enough
You are
Not
Alone
Within you is everything
Everything you need to feel complete
To feel content
And everything else is a compliment
A blessing

Make it
Take it
Indulge in you
Let your true substance pour out now
A.L.O.N.E.
You are everything but...

– Alone With Company

Dear Moon,
You are my lover & friend
Never leaving me unsatisfied always there to brighten up my
dark sky
Always shining down a new light
A new hope
You take my breath away every time
Your solitude brings a new peace
A piece of adventure

Love From,
A Soul Down Below
X

– Dear Moon

The beginning & the end
A real destination
Undeniably, the most powerful source of light we possess
Plant seeds of love
And watch them radiate beauty back into the earth

– Love

We were meant to meet today!
Content
Stable
Happy
Loved
Peaceful
Made it
Successful
Accomplished...
What does that feel like?

We live in a whirlwind where the more we have, the more we want
But success will never taste as sweet if we never cherish the journey
Sometimes we need to discover a new appreciation for life
So let us take a bite of life now
And taste all the lessons
All the joys
And smile

Because everything happens in a pattern
To paint a unique picture
To me
To you
It will all add up in the end
To create a special equation
A special answer

But...
Let us
Smile
Because no matter where we're coming from
We were meant to meet today
To discover a new way
A new strength!
Together
Me
You
Have a new way to go now...

– *The Timing Of Life*

Next destination, I can see your light shining from amongst
the clouds
I can feel your warm embrace
It's been a while since I felt love
Touched love
I miss it

Commonly, we miss what we don't have
And I am tired of missing
Tired of seeking
So maybe it's time to stop...
Stop seeking what I don't have and just be!

Time is a master at creating a masterpiece
I must learn to sit back and take notes
Be a perfect student during these lessons
And prepare for the next journey
Because every lesson has a message
So, let us tune in and listen
I wait on your arrival...
Next destination.

– Above & Beyond The Clouds

Freedom is you
Freedom is me
Freedom is us
Freedom is we
Free
Freedom
Free
Freedom!

Like the sun we rise up
So, let us break the shackles on our mind
Elevate to a state so high
Beyond Empire State
Beyond Everest
Beyond!

Let us break out of these walls!
No limits can bind us
No past can pull us back
So, let calamity transform us
Transport us to a new level

Freedom is you
Freedom is me
Freedom is us
Freedom is we!

Fear is in the past
Because faith is present
Let us march out
Speak out
Get ready for victory

Fallen down
But risen again
The trails came to knock us out
But his power took on the next round
And a sound of victory poured out!

He has already won our race
So, don't fight for freedom
Be free because...

Freedom is you
Freedom is me
Freedom is us
Freedom is we
Free
Freedom!

The father above is our anchor
He will cover our minds
Body
Soul
Because he is our keeper
He is our keeper

Freedom is me
Freedom is you
Freedom is us
Freedom is we
Free
Freedom
Free
Freedom!

– Freedom Is Now

Gabrielle Hibbert

I rest in God's assurance
Even when the curtains calls
I never fall
Because I rest in his assurance

He is the anchor of my soul
Keeping my spirits calm in the midst of the storm
I rest in his assurance

My flesh failed me
Crumbled when I was weak
Under intense heat
My mind collapsed
But God's grace gave me life again
So I rest in his assurance!

Always
Saves
Secures
Understands
Rescues
Able
Never fails
Calms
Eternal

As I rest in God's assurance
All things are possible!

My palms open wide
Ready to receive his gifts
Waiting to catch his wisdom
And to be led down a path of purpose

I lift everything up to him
To restore
Renew
Rebuild
All!

It's his call now
So I rest in God's assurance.

– *God's Assurance*

Faith is my heart beat, keeping this failing flesh from falling.

Faith
Fly freely
And take me to a new land
To a new home
To restoration

When all walls are crumbling and the ground beneath me is
shaking
Faith is my heart beat, keeping me from falling

In the middle of a fire, when my mind is consumed
And my insides are burning
Faith is my heart beat, keeping me from falling

Faith
Fly freely
And take me to a new land
To a new home
To restoration

When anxiety strikes and shakes all parts of me
Faith is my heart beat, keeping me from falling

When humans fail and hurt me when I am weak
Faith is my heart beat, keeping me from falling

Faith
Fly freely
And take me to a new land
To a new home
To restoration

I know every season has a reason
Every test has a testimony
And throughout it all
My faith restores my soul

So trust him
Have faith
For faith will never fail but sustain you!

– Faith

Open her book
It's a pathway to her heart
Her soul
Each page bursting with wisdom and life
Capturing each eye
Creating a unique picture

Open her book and set her soul free
Ready to be vulnerable
Ready to be open

Tears will fall
Words of rage may jump off the page
Lines will blur
As you lose yourself
Delve deeper and find her
Dark, enriching, intriguing

– *Openbook, Opensoul*

Acknowledgements

Firstly, I give all the glory to God for this creative work and for turning my pain into purpose. I thank God for giving me boldness to be open and share my battles with the world. I thank Him for giving me the gift of writing, so I can connect, empower and heal with my words. I will continue to use this art form for His greater purpose!

A very special thank you to all my family & friends who have kept me motivated with their encouraging words and shared loved during the difficult times. I thank God for such special souls, may he bless you all. A special thank you to my sister Rochelle and Hyphon Music Group for designing the cover of this book and all their creative expertise throughout this journey.

Thank you to all my young mentees who have kept me focused and encouraged me to publish. I thank God our paths crossed and may you all continue to pursue your dreams.

Thank you to Conscious Dreams Publishing for your guidance and believing in my story.

About the Author

Open Book, Open Soul is Gabrielle's first collection of poetry and prose.

Gabrielle views her life as a creative flow and believes that the most beautiful flowers blossom in the darkest rooms.

She first discovered her love for poetry whilst studying English Literature at University. Since then, poetry has empowered and inspired her to express herself through writing.

'Expression not suppression'...throughout the growing pains of life writing created a safe space for Gabrielle. Through her writing, she engages with love, loss, trauma, identity, healing, womanhood, mental health and social issues.

Her active work as a Youth Mentor has driven Gabrielle to share her journey and creativity with the young people. She has since brought her performative poetry to stages, colleges, charity organisations and churches across London. Gabrielle aims to continue this writing journey and use her gifts to spread hope and healing around the world.